MONSTER

-SURVIVAL GUIDE-

Written by Heather Dakota

Illustrated by Left Side Down and Ali Castro

Designed by Ali Castro, Daniel Jankowski,
and Bill Henderson

Tangerine Press
an imprint of
SCHOLASTIC
www.scholastic.com

P9-CCV-747

TABLE OF CONTENTS

Dear Reader,

As a child, I was fascinated by stories of monsters, real and imaginary. I was sure that Bigfoot lived in the woods behind my house. In fact, I'm pretty sure my next-door neighbor was a vampire. Often, I was met with puzzled looks from adults. They wanted proof, not just stories.

As I got older, I also wanted the facts. If these monsters were real, I wanted to prove it to myself and others. If they weren't, I wanted that known, too. In this modern age, it should be easy to unlock the secrets of the monsters that plague your nightmares. However, it's not that simple.

That's why I've written this book. Inside are a few of my monster-hunting adventures over the last couple of years and notes on what it takes to hunt these monsters on your own. It takes math and science, as well as tracking and survival skills, to get the evidence needed to convince a skeptic of the existence of these monsters. I'm always looking for a monster-hunting apprentice to join the team. Are you up for the challenge? If you are, then read on!

Sincerely,

HEATHER DAKOTA

Monster Hunter

BIGFOOT

OCTOBER 15, 2011

I headed out of camp before dawn in search of the elusive Bigfoot, also known as Sasquatch. There have been thousands of sightings, but no one has been able to get a good photograph or conclusive evidence that this creature even exists. I'm skeptical, but ready for an adventure.

BIGFOOT CASE FILE

This hominid creature lives in the forests of the Pacific Northwest in the U.S. and Canada. Bigfoot is described as a large, hairy bipedal creature. It is approximately 7 ft. (2.1 m) tall and weighs approximately 500 lbs. (227 kg). The hair is typically dark brown or a dark reddish color. Witnesses describe large eyes, a pronounced brow, and a low-set forehead. The top of the head is described as crested, similar to that of the male gorilla. The foot size is 24 in. (60 cm) long and 8 in. (20 cm) wide—that's larger than Shaquille O'Neal's foot!

There are no fossil records of a large hominid in North America, nor have any remains of a Bigfoot creature ever been found...yet.

The Legend

Stories from the indigenous tribes of the Pacific Northwest existed before the creature was actually named. Details differ slightly, but similar stories tell of a large, wild creature that lived in the mountains. In 1958, a set of large footprints were found in Northern California and a plaster cast was made of the prints. The story was published in the Humboldt Times with a photo of the crew holding one of the casts. Everyone had been calling the track maker "Big Foot," but a newspaper reporter shortened the name to "Bigfoot." Both scientists and Bigfoot believers agree that many of the sightings are hoaxes or misidentified animals.

How to Survive in
THE PACIFIC NORTHWEST

When searching for Bigfoot, be ready for the tough weather conditions of the Pacific Northwest. This area is known for its rainy weather, so you'll need to take precautions. The important thing is to stay as dry as possible. So, be prepared to get wet!

Looking for Bigfoot: Supplies

- **GEAR**
- **ROPES**
- **MOTION-ACTIVATED CAMERAS**
- **WATERPROOF TENT**

- **TARP**
- **SLEEPING BAG**
  If a down sleeping bag gets wet, it will be worthless. Choose a synthetic bag.

- **WATER**
  You need 1 gal. (3.7 l) for each day you're out in the wild. That's water for drinking and cleaning up.

- **FOOD**

- **CAMP STOVE**

- **DISHES & UTENSILS**

- **TRASH BAGS & PLASTIC BAGS**

- **DUCT TAPE**
  All-purpose item

- **COTTON BALLS** soaked in Vaseline in a plastic bag— works great as a fire starter!

- **FLASHLIGHT**

- **JOURNAL & PEN**

- **CLOTHES**
  Rain jacket & pants

- **WATERPROOF HIKING BOOTS**

- **WOOL SOCKS**

- **SYNTHETIC UNDERWEAR**
  No cotton! Once cotton gets wet, it will stay cold and clammy against your skin.

- **SYNTHETIC, WARM PANTS AND SHIRTS**
  Jeans and cotton t-shirts ake a long time to dry.

The Pacific Northwest is wet, all the time. I need to brush up on my survival skills if I want to stay dry out here.

Surviving a BIGFOOT ATTACK

WHAT YOU DO:

Bigfoot is a very large creature. It's even taller than most NBA players. So what's a tiny human to do?

Bigfoot is territorial by nature, just like bears. The good news is, that unless provoked, Bigfoot won't attack. It'll be more afraid of you than you are of it. Maybe. Keep in mind that wild animals are unpredictable. Keep your distance and do not approach or startle the big creature.

If you do startle it, running won't do any good. Some believe that Bigfoot can run at 35 mph (56 kph) in open areas. This means you can't outrun it. Your best bet is to head for the woods and zigzag through the trees. Whatever you do, watch where you're going!

We are hot on the trail of a large, bipedal creature.

I saw it late last night, and the stench was awful. Motion-activated cameras have been set up just outside of camp with food (berries and meat) as bait. If an animal crosses the cameras' sensors, we will have our conclusive proof.

It jumped out from behind a tree, right in front of me. It must have been stalking me for miles. I narrowly escaped, but I was right! Zigzagging through the trees was the only way of outrunning this massive creature. It tired much more quickly than I did.

WE FOUND THIS IN THE WOODS. LOOKS LIKE A BIGFOOT HAND TO ME.

CAMERA ON MOTION SENSOR CAUGHT THIS IMAGE

HISTORIC PHOTO OF BIGFOOT

IT DOES EXIST!

Here is the evidence that we collected on the hunt in the pacific northwest.

FEBRUARY 8, 2015

While on vacation in Yellowstone National Park, a young family caught what appears to be a family of Bigfoot on video. The three-and-a-half minute video shows several bison roaming and eating grass in the foreground. Then, all of a sudden, four dark figures come out from behind a group of trees.

Park officials are unconvinced by the footage. However, Bigfoot believers point out that the creatures' bodily dimensions, gait, and speed are entirely inhuman in nature.

PHOTO CAPTURED BY OUR MOTION SENSOR CAMERA

BIGFOOT HAIR FOUND ON A BUSH

YETI

NOVEMBER 8, 2012

We landed in Kathmandu, Nepal, to begin our adventure. From there it was a short but bumpy bus ride to Namche Bazaar, where we would begin our 22-day trek. It was important to make sure that we were not in the Annapurna region during the heavy tourist season, but we didn't want to be caught in the heavy snows of winter, either. We hired our sherpa and were off in search of the Yeti.

Yetis are thought to inhabit the mountain regions of Russia, China, and Nepal. All accounts say the Yeti is covered with white or clear fur with dark skin (like a polar bear). It stands approximately 6 ft. (1.8 m) tall and weighs about 200 to 400 lbs. (90-180 kg). It likes to eat yak and sheep.

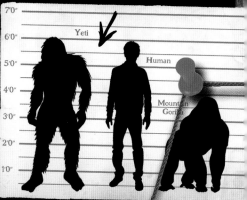

The word "Yeti" comes from the Tibetan name for the creature yeh-teh, which translates to "Rock Bear."

The Legend

L.A. Waddell, an explorer, reported finding unusual footprints in the 1800s. The prints looked more like ape feet than bear tracks. With so many Western mountain climbers coming to the region in the 1900s, the stories of the mysterious animal grew. While on an expedition, in 1925, a Greek photographer sighted a bipedal creature. At 15,000 ft. (4,572 m), snow covered the ground and weather conditions were frigid. While descending the mountain, the expedition found what they thought were the creature's footprints, describing them as similar in shape to those of a man, but only 6 to 7 in. (15 cm to 17.5 cm) long by 4 in. (10.2 cm) wide at the broadest part of the foot. The footprints had five distinct toes and the insteps were perfectly clear.

How to Survive a HIMALAYAN BLIZZARD

Heavy snow is falling. There's thunder and lightning, and the constant rumble of avalanches everywhere. This is the type of survival situation where you could live or die based on your decisions. Being unprepared is not an option.

DON'T LEAVE HOME WITHOUT:

- COMPASS
- ROPE
- WATER BOTTLES
- WIND-PROOF JACKET
- 2 LAYERS OF SOCKS
- MERINO WOOL THERMALS
- FLEECE PANTS AND SHIRT

- DOWN JACKET
- TREKKING PANTS
- WATERPROOF JACKET
- TREKKING BOOTS
- SILK HAND LINERS
- GLOVES
- WALKING POLES

- MOISTURIZER
- LIP BALM
- HAND SANITIZER
- SNACKS
- UV SUNGLASSES
  The UV is very strong at 16,000 ft. (5,000 m).
- HEAD LAMP
- HAT

RULES FOR SURVIVING
SNOW-COVERED MOUNTAINS

1. Check your own gear. Don't rely on someone else to do it for you.

2. Respect the weather. The changes in weather at high altitudes are often fast and unforgiving. One minute the sun is shining and the next you're snow blind, the wind is freezing, and you can't feel your fingers and toes.

3. Use the ropes. Clip in everywhere!

4. Drink plenty of water. High altitudes and dehydration can cause headaches, frostbite, water retention, and confusion.

5. Know how to make a fire.

6. Bring a tarp for emergency shelter. If you have found shelter, stay there.

7. Get fit and train before you head out into the high mountain passes of the Himalayas.

8. Hire a respected Sherpa (Guide).

lizzards and snow-covered mountains are nothing compared to actually coming face-to-face with a Yeti. But, if you're not prepared to deal with the ice, you certainly don't stand chance. I didn't bring the right gear on my last trip, and I almost lost my toes to frostbite! This time, I'm determined to see the creature without freezing to death.

17

Well, a blizzard came in and completely ruined the cameras. At least we found Yeti footprints all over the mountains by the yak bait. We had to move quickly before the weather turned, but we managed to make casts of the print before it started snowing, again.

YETI
FOOTPRINT

Want to make your own **Yeti** print cast?
Here's how we do it in the field.

WHAT YOU NEED:

- **PLASTER OF PARIS**
- **MIXING CONTAINER** (an old yogurt or butter tub will work)
- **WATER**
- **PAPER CLIP**
- **CARDBOARD** strip (long enough to go completely around the track)

WHAT YOU DO:

1. Use the cardboard strip to build a wall around the track. Hold it together with the paper clip. Gently, press the strip into the soil so the plaster won't run out from under it when you pour the plaster of Paris.

2. Mix the plaster of Paris with 2 parts plaster dust to one part water. For a large print, that would be 2 cups (473 g) to 1 cup (235 ml) water. Add the plaster to the water all at the same time and stir it together. It should be thick like pancake batter, and make sure you get all the lumps out. It will take 2-3 minutes.

NOTE: The plaster will begin to set as soon as it comes in contact with the water, so work quickly.

3. Tap the mixing container on the ground to remove any bubbles.

4. Carefully pour the plaster into the prepared mold. Do not pour the plaster directly into the track. It is better to pour it off to the side and let it run into the track. Start with the finer details.

5. Once you are done pouring and have filled in all of the details, let the track set for at least 30 minutes. Be patient. As the plaster dries, it will look dull instead of glossy.

6. After the 30 minutes, gently touch the surface of the cast. If it is still soft, give it another 10 minutes or so. Don't press too hard or you could crack the cast. If it is dry to the touch, gently tap on it with your knuckles. If it is firm, then it is safe to remove the cast.

7. Pick it up by reaching underneath and lifting it up. Do not try to lift it with a stick. That could damage the cast. The cast will have dirt and twigs on it. Leave them for now.

8. Allow the cast to dry for several more days before cleaning it. Don't wrap it in a plastic bag. This prevents the moisture from escaping.

YAK, YETI'S FAVORITE FOOD

YETI CLAW, FOUND NEAR A DEAD YAK

YETI JAWBONE

YETI FOOTPRINT FOUND IN THE SNOW.

Scientists at Oxford University in England have DNA proof of a bearlike creature that has been extinct since the Ice Age. The two hair samples were taken from a remote region in the Himalayas.

WE FOUND IT

Our Sherpa guide has led us to the last place that he
spotted the creature. We have set a series of cameras
near the strange footprints we found last week, with
yak meat as bait. We'll get a photo this time, unless
the snows move in and blinds the cameras' sensors.
Fortunately, we found a lot of evidence on our last trip
that supports the existence of Yeti.

WEREWOLF

MAY 27, 2010

We are about to begin our search for a Werewolf that has been spotted in Cannock Chase, an area near Staffordshire, England. Although beautiful by day, the forests have been the place of more than 21 reported sightings of a Werewolf, the most recent in 2009. All of the witnesses gave the same description. They saw what looked like a large dog. But as they got closer, the creature pulled itself up on its hind legs and ran into the forest. We'll certainly have our hands full tonight. It's the full moon.

WEREWOLF CASE FILE

Werewolves are humans with the ability to change into a wolf or a wolf-human. Sometimes this change happens by choice and other times by uncontrollable forces, like by the light of the full moon. These often out-of-control, large beings are often hungry and driven to kill whatever stands in their path, including humans. When a Werewolf wakes up in the morning, it cannot remember anything that happened in the wolf form.

8'0"

Alaskan
Brown Bear

Werewolf

7'0"

6'0"

Human

5'0"

4'0"

3'0"

2'0"

1'0"

Werewolf translates to
"man-wolf."

The Legend

The legend of the Werewolf is one of the oldest on Earth. No one is sure where the legend actually started, because it has its roots in many different cultures. One indigenous tribe in the U.S. may have received the gift of the Werewolf. In the 1500s, several people claimed to be able to transform into Werewolves and kill innocent people. Becoming a Werewolf was thought to be brought on by witches, so many of the people who were convicted of being a Werewolf were put to death.

How to Survive a Cold Night in the WOODS

You find yourself alone in the woods on a cold night. What do you do? Panic is not a good answer. The best thing to do is prepare. Here's how.

PREPARE, JUST IN CASE

1. **Eat something before you leave,** no matter how long you think you'll be gone.

2. **Know where you're going and when you'll be back.** Give this information to someone who is not going with you.

3. **Learn how to use a compass.** Remember: the sun rises in the east and sets in the west.

4. **Don't panic if you get lost.** Stop, sit down, and prepare for survival by gathering material.

5. **Know where you are.** Find a way to mark a tree, rock, or anything else that can be seen at a distance.

6. **Stay in one place.** This increases your chances of being found.

7. **Seek shade.**

8. **Signal your location by making noise**. Use the whistle. Three short blasts of the whistle is the universal distress call. Or use the mirror to catch the light three times.

9. **Find a good source of water, but don't stray too far from your original spot**. Remember, do not drink water directly from the stream. This can make you very sick. Be sure to use the water purifying tablets before drinking. Know how to use them.

10. **Make a shelter**. An A-frame is the easiest shelter to make. Use fallen branches, leaves, and other plants to close in as much of your shelter as possible. Don't use too much energy to make your shelter or you'll become exhausted.

11. **Find safe food**. Eat your snacks first, but ration them out.

12. **Bundle up in your space blanket at night**. You don't want hypothermia to set in.

DON'T LEAVE HOME WITHOUT...

- **Backpack**
- **Water bottle**
- **Snacks**
- **Whistle**
- **Space blanket**
- **Signaling mirror**
- **Water purifying tablets**
- **Compass**
- **550 paracord**
- **First aid kit**
- **Cell phone** with a spare battery or a portable CB radio

Don't do what I did and forget a pack when you're out monster hunting. I left everything at the hotel just for a quick walk on the moors after dinner. I got lost. It was cold and wet. And there was no way for me to build a fire. It didn't help to hear the Werewolf howling in the distance.

PROTECT
Yourself from a Werewolf

Put a river between you and the Werewolf. They don't like to cross water.

A branch from a yew tree

Silver jewelry

If you want to be a monster hunter, you'll need a few things to help keep you safe from **Werewolves**.

A piece of mistletoe

Wolfsbane Potion

However, if you are an expert monster hunter, here's what you do: grind up the wolfsbane root and boil it. Filter the water through cloth to remove the root pieces. Bottle the potion in a small vial. When confronted with a Werewolf, uncork the vial and toss the water on the werewolf. If you are just beginning your monster-hunting career, practice with plain water and a few drops of blue food coloring.

WARNING:
Wolfsbane Potion is extremely dangerous.

I came right up on the Werewolf.

This time I had everything that I needed, including my wolfsbane. The Werewolf growled as it approached me, but I stood my ground. It howled and attacked! Bam! I tossed the wolfsbane on it. I didn't even look back. I made it back to the hotel in no time.

MANAGED TO GET A HAND OFF A WEREWOLF

THE WEREWOLF WAS COMING RIGHT AT ME

CONFIRMED WEREWOLF FUR

There are several real medical conditions that mimic the look of a **W**erewolf. **O**ne is hypertrichosis (hy-per-tri-**KOH**-sis), which creates really long hair on the face and body. **T**he other condition is porphyria (pawr-**FEER**-ee-uh), which makes people extremely sensitive to light, and causes seizures, anxiety, and other symptoms. **T**hese are both rare conditions, but could they have fed the **W**erewolf legends?

It was Howling All Night!

The creature was howling all night. Fear was running rampant among our group, but we found the evidence we needed without anyone getting hurt.

WAY TOO CLOSE TO A WEREWOLF!

MOTION SENSOR CAMERA IMAGE

WEREWOLF CANINE TOOTH

HUMAN CANINE TOOTH

VAMPIRE

JANUARY 20, 2013

Vampire hunting is best left to the professionals. And there is no better than the great-great-great-granddaughter of Professor Abraham Van Helsing, the most famous Vampire hunter of all time. I have to admit, I'm a little star-struck to be in the presence of such a famous monster hunter.

Anyway, we find ourselves in London, England, near the famous Highgate Cemetery. We will set up our investigation in a few hours. I must go and get the equipment ready.

8'0"	
7'0"	Alaskan Brown Bear
Vampire	
6'0"	Bat
5'0"	Human
4'0"	
3'0"	
2'0"	
1'0"	

VAMPIRE CASE FILE

Vampires are cold-blooded, blood-thirsty killers, despite the stories you've read. It is generally believed that Vampires are undead beings who crave blood. They often have pale skin and are sensitive to sunlight and other bright lights. Therefore, they sleep during the day. Vampires tend to have red eyes, long fingers, toenails, bad breath, and long canine teeth. Some have been known to have super-human strength.

The Legend

Almost every culture on Earth has a Vampire legend. The stories about each Vampire are different, but there are many common threads. Vampire stories became popular in the early 1800s, when superstitions began to filter into Western Europe from Romania and Greece. It has been reported that villagers in Russia found several dead cows and sheep in the village. This led to several villagers looking for evidence of vampirism. They found holes in the earth near a grave. When they dug up the corpse, it looked healthy with no signs of decomposition and had fresh blood around the lips.

31

It was a Close Call!

We began our research in Highgate Cemetery. Just as I was passing the gates a tall, shadowy figure swept past me. I turned quickly, but the fog was too thick to see through. As I was walking through the cemetery, I could feel someone watching me. Then, the hair on the back of my neck stood on end as someone grabbed me from behind and threw me to the ground. I let out a blood-curdling scream. Van Helsing came running with her Vampire-hunting kit, but it was too late. The figure disappeared into the fog.

THE BACKGROUND: The cemetery was built in London, England, in 1839. According to several reports, a tall figure with red eyes was spotted in the area in the 1960s and again in 1971. This time a young girl passing the cemetery was attacked by a tall, white-faced, dark figure that threw her to the ground. Lucky for this girl, a car pulled up to the scene and the shadowy figure fled. Her story supported other sightings in the area, which continue to this day.

IT BIT ME! Fortunately, Van Helsing had heard of ways to treat Vampire bites. I was game for anything, but now we were up against the clock. We had to get back to the hotel within 30 minutes, or there was no reversing the effects of the bite. Every second we delayed was bringing me closer to becoming a Vampire myself.

Van Helsing began treatment immediately, and the severe pain, sleepiness, and light sensitivity began to fade. The swelling around the bite lasted for days, but with the help of Van Helsing, this treatment saved my life.

How to Treat a
VAMPIRE BITE

While we know that the bite of a Vampire can be deadly, there are ways to treat the bite that may help the victim and stop the poison from spreading. You have about 15-30 minutes before the effects cannot be reversed.

DETERMINE IF IT IS A VAMPIRE BITE OR SOME OTHER CREEPY CRAWLY.

- Are there fang marks?
- Is there severe localized pain?
- Is the person weak and sleepy?
- Does there seem to be a sensitivity to light?
- Are the canine teeth beginning to grow longer?

TREAT THE BITE

Apply a wrap about 4 in. (5 cm to 10 cm) above the bite to slow the spread of the Vampire's poison. The wrap should be loose enough to slip a finger underneath it.

- Attempt to draw out the poison with a suction cup.
- Wash the bite with soap and water.
- Keep the victim calm and quiet.
- Cover the area with a compress of cool filtered water mixed with garlic.
- Monitor the heartbeat. If it stops, the victim may be turning into a Vampire.

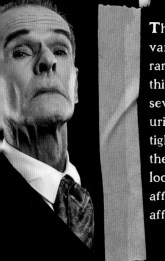

There is a real disease that mimics vampirism. Porphyric hemophilia is a rare genetic disorder. The symptoms of this disorder include: sensitivity to light, severe abdominal pain, purplish-red urine, increased hair growth, and skin tightening (when it happens around the mouth it will make the canine teeth look like fangs). This disorder also affects the iron in the blood, making the affected person crave more blood.

Create a
VAMPIRE-
HUNTING KIT

Every professional vampire hunter needs the tools of the trade to hunt the blood-sucking undead. Emma Van Helsing has graciously allowed me to photograph her tool kit, which has been passed down through the generations in her family.

Garlic to repel a Vampire

Leather-covered box to hold your tools

Mirror to check for a reflection. Vampires don't have a reflection.

Flashlight to see in the dark

This is the most important kit for hunting Vampires. When I first started out, I only had the stakes. This means you have to get really close to a Vampire. I wish I had bought the coffin nails first.

Holy water to kill a Vampire

Vintage coffin nails to nail the vampire in its coffin

4 wooden crosses sharpened into daggers to be hammered into the vampire's heart

Large wooden mallet for hammering in the stakes

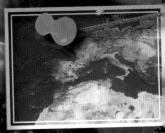

LOCH NESS MONSTER

MAY 2, 2011

We've just arrived at our cottage on the shores of Loch Ness in Scotland, with a beautiful view of the loch. The cozy accommodations are just big enough for our gear and the crew. After our full Scottish breakfast, which includes oatcakes with homemade jam, yogurt with fruit, tea, Scottish oatmeal, toast, broiled tomato with cheese on top, rasher of bacon (or ham), potato tattie, banger (sausage), mushrooms, baked beans, one egg, and black pudding, we plan to do some investigating on the loch, but first, a nap!

LOCH NESS MONSTER CASE FILE

The Loch Ness Monster, or Nessie, is supposed to resemble an extinct plesiosaur. It has a long neck, horse-like head, and humped back. It is dark gray in color. Nessie is approximately 15 ft. to 40 ft. (4.5 m to 12 m) long and weighs about 2,500 lbs. (1,134 kg). The loch itself is 23 mi. (37 km) long and about 1 mi. (1.6 km) wide. At its deepest point, it is 786 ft. (240 m) deep. It is one of the largest bodies of fresh water in Britain.

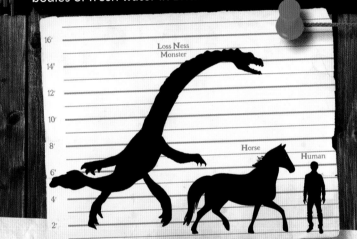

The Legend

This lake monster is one of the most famous in the world. Some believe that it is a dinosaur that swam into the lake before it became landlocked. The first reported sighting was in AD 565. According to legend, St. Columba turned away a giant beast that was threatening a man in the Ness River, which flows into the lake. The first photo of Nessie, as the monster is commonly called, was published in the Daily Mail on April 21, 1934. The photograph was taken by a London surgeon. The story spread with the occasional photograph or sighting, but no hard evidence has been found on the lake bottom or washed ashore.

IT WAS FULL OF TOURISTS!

It was very difficult to find any evidence of the Loch Ness Monster. It looks like the area has been picked clean. The whole place is mobbed with people hoping to get a glimpse of the monster. The hunt was entirely disappointing. At least we found a few things.

KRAKEN SCALES
FOUND FLOATING
ON THE SURFACE OF
LOCH NESS

TEETH FOUND ALONG
THE SHORELINE OF
LOCH NESS

HISTORIC PHOTO OF
LOCH NESS MONSTER, 1934

I SAW THE CLASSIC HUMP!

Our expedition had already come to an end, and I was disappointed that it had not yielded the evidence that we needed. Frustrated, I decided to take a stroll along the lake shore and ponder my next move. When all of a sudden, out of the corner of my eye, I caught a ripple on the smooth water. That's when I saw it! Luckily, I kept my wits about me and snapped a few photos. Unfortunately, my hands were shaking so bad, I'm not sure I did myself any favors. I can only tell you what I saw. We'll extend our stay by a few days to see if we can find more evidence.

How could Nessie Survive?

Loch Ness is a cold, deep lake with steeply sloping shores. So, how could a 65-million-year-old dinosaur survive for this long? Good question!

1. If Nessie is a carnivore, there are plenty of fish in the loch, including salmon, charr, eels, pike, and trout. Mammals also swim the lake, including deer and otters.

2. There could be very few of these creatures, only enough to keep the species alive but elude capture.

3. Nessie is a warm-blooded animal. Warm-blooded animals can maintain their body temperature.

4. It is possible that Nessie is a plankton feeder, like a basking shark. However, the Loch Ness Monster has been seen going after fish. In the top 100 ft. (30 m), there is approximately 1 ton (900 kg) of fish. This number does not include eels, which could also be part of the monster's diet.

5. The loch is very dark, especially the deeper you go. If the Loch Ness Monster feeds on fish and eels at a greater depth, it would have eyes like an owl's.

I didn't get a clear photograph, but based on eyewitness reports I think this might be the monster's overall shape.

After spotting the monster in the lake, I decided to go for a row in order to get a better set of photos. A few hours in, I heard (and felt) a sharp crack from underneath the boat. Was Nessie attacking me? I was almost thrown headfirst into the lake! Then, just as suddenly, the water became calm again. Of course, I wasn't ready, and the camera fell straight into the depths of the lake. Next time, I'll handle things differently. I'm still not sure what hit my boat...

How to Survive a
LOCH NESS
MONSTER ATTACK

There has never been a confirmed report of **N**essie attacking anyone, so it's not likely that you'll be attacked. **H**owever, monsters are unpredictable, so here's what you do, and what **I** should have done when it happened to me.

1. Take a deep breath. Are you sure it's Nessie?

2. If you're in a boat or on a paddle board, hang on. Nessie may think you're a fish. Once it finds out that you're not its food, it may leave you alone.

3. If you're on the shore, move as far back as possible. It is unlikely that Nessie will come on shore.

4. This lake is VERY cold. Make sure you have a wet suit on. It's more likely that you'd die from hypothermia than by a Loch Ness Monster attack.

5. Have your camera ready. No one has ever gotten a clear photo of this monster.

SWAMP APE
or Skunk Ape

SEPTEMBER 4, 2012

We thought this was going to be a leisurely vacation, but that wasn't the case. Within a few hours of arriving in Orlando, we received a call reporting a Swamp Ape sighting on the Northern edge of the Florida Everglades. We are gathering our equipment and will head out within the hour. A monster hunter's work is never done.

7'0" Swamp Ape
6'0"
'0"
'0"
'0"
0"
0"

Alaskan Brown Bear

Human

Mountain Gorilla

SWAMP APE CASE FILE

The Swamp Ape is allegedly a distant relative of Bigfoot. It has a strong odor that smells like rotting garbage, methane, or, as its name implies, a skunk. The average Swamp Ape stand 6 to 7 ft. (1.8 to 2.1 m) tall and weighs about 250 lbs. (113 kg). The creature is covered in reddish-black hair and closely resembles an orangutan. Castings of the footprints show four toes on each foot. From stool samples, it looks like it eats birds, wild hogs, and berries.

The Legend

Sightings of the Swamp Ape started hundreds of years ago, but sightings hit a peak in the 1960s and '70s. In the 1970s, the sightings became so common, everyone thought that it was a matter of time before one was caught. In December 2000, a concerned woman sent a letter to the Sarasota County Sheriff's Office, claiming the "orangutan" in the enclosed photos could cause a car accident if it weren't caught soon. The Swamp Ape sightings continue to this day, but little evidence has been found.

BONE FRAGMENTS
FOUND IN SWAMP

SWAMP APE CAPTURED
BY MOTION SENSOR CAMERA

THE STENCH WAS UNBELIEVABLE!

We got as close as I want to get to this monster.
The smell is unbelievably horrible. I've smelled skunk
before. This is definitely worse. Grabbing a gas mask and
heading back out in the field. We are definitely close!

SWAMPS OF THE SOUTHERN US, THOUGHT TO BE THE HOME OF SWAMP APE

A SKUNK APE APPEARS IN FLORIDA SWAMP

FEBRUARY 1, 2015

In the murky, swamp of the Hillsborough River outside of Tampa, Florida, a man and his best friend were out fishing in their canoe. About 1:00 in the afternoon, the two men heard a noise and saw movement in the trees. One of them grabbed his cell phone and started videotaping. Initially, they thought it was a bear, but it was playing in the water, trying to grab something. One of them moved the paddle, which startled the creature. Then, the hairy beast moved off into the swamp.

A zoologist who examined the video said, "The mannerisms of the subject appear to be very apelike in behavior. It dips its hand down into the water and brings it up. This is not bear behavior."

While the evidence seems inconclusive, the two men say there is a good chance they saw a Skunk Ape.

SWAMP APE FUR, FOUND NEAR THE CAMERAS

How to Survive in the
SWAMP

Beware of these swamp dangers ...

1. Snakes
2. Bogs
3. Alligators
4. High humidity
5. High temperatures & sunburn
6. Mosquitoes & other biting insects
7. Lack of water suitable for drinking
8. Poisonous fumes

As we were hunting for the Skunk Ape, we were constantly bitten by mosquitoes, saw numerous alligators and snakes, and quickly ran out of water. Skunk Ape hunting is no joke! Make sure you follow these instructions, and learn from my mistakes.

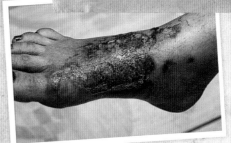

Trench foot is a condition that will become worse if not treated properly. **T**he feet may become numb and turn red or blue. **T**rench foot can be prevented by keeping the feet clean, warm, and dry.

There is a lot of danger in a swamp.

- Seek shelter. Climbing a tree will keep you from becoming an alligator's latest meal.

- Find dry firewood, fallen branches, palm fronds. Everything must be dry.

- Place stones around your fire pit to prevent the fire from escaping and causing a swamp fire.

- Don't drink the swamp water directly. You'll need to use your shirt as a filter. Then, boil it over your fire to kill the bacteria.

- Keep moving west or east in the daylight. Check your movement by the sun.

- Avoid all rivers or deep sections of water.

- Stop occasionally to dry your feet and shoes to avoid trench foot.

Make sure you can read a map.

How to Bait a
SWAMP APE

Think long and hard about catching one of these creatures. **T**he smell is gagging! **H**ere are some things to keep in mind.

- Researchers have found some success with lima beans as bait, but other dry beans work well, too, including black-eyed peas, pinto beans, and kidney beans—as well as corn and rice. You'll need 1 lb. (0.45 kg).

- Head to higher points where the Swamp Ape feeds. They like to hang out in the cypress.

- Watch out for spiders, snakes, Florida panthers, and alligators.

- Keep track of where you're going. There are more than 1.5 million acres in the Everglades.

- Head out at sunset.

- Choose your spot. Set up your camera with the motion sensor.

- Clear an area about 10 sq. ft. (0.9 sq. m). Remove all dead leaves and grasses. Loosen the top soil.

- Spread your bait near and in front of your camera and do a test shot of yourself.

- Head back to your camp for a good night's sleep.

- Go back to see if you have the perfect photo of the Swamp Ape.

NOTE: Baiting is strictly prohibited in national parks and state-owned preserves.

We set up our camera and waited in the hunting blind. It came up behind us, lurking behind the large cypress trees. We stayed as quiet as we could. The sound of footsteps in puddles came closer and closer. It could smell us and we could definitely smell it. Pee-yew!

As it stepped into the clearing, we got a good look at it. That's when I shifted positions and stepped on my pencil. Our motion sensor cameras went off at the same time and scared it back into the swamp.

CHUPACABRA

JULY 5, 2012

There have been a lot of sightings in the last couple of years in Texas. There is some pretty good video footage as well. We're meeting with the South Texas police officer who captured the latest video. The hunt for this elusive creature will begin tomorrow on the Dalton family ranch, where hundreds of cows have been killed, mysteriously drained of blood.

CHUPACABRA CASE FILE

The Chupacabra is about the size of a dog, but with a strange profile. It typically has red skin, red oval eyes, fangs, claws, and spinal quills or possibly coarse hair on its back. Chupacabras tend to have a strange, deep growl, not like any other animal you've ever heard.

Human

Goat

Chupacabra

CHUPACABRA is Spanish for "goat sucker."

The Legend

In 1995 in Puerto Rico, 150 farm animals were killed in a single summer, giving birth to the legend of the Chupacabra. All of the farm animals had been mysteriously drained of blood. By the late 1990s, the creature had been spotted in Texas, Florida, and Mexico.

DEAD COWS FOUND IN A PATH OF DESTRUCTION

FUR SAMPLE FROM A CHUPACABRA

ALL OF THE ANIMALS WERE KILLED!

Something is definitely fishy here. We're looking for this monster on a small farm in South Texas, where there have been a lot of sightings over the last couple of years. This evidence we found is amazing, but I'm starting to suspect the beast is not a monster at all...

SOLVED

THE CAPTURED
CHUPACABRA

CLAW SAMPLES
PULLED FROM
THE DEAD COWS

CHUPACABRA
MYSTERY SOLVED!

The Chupacabra mystery seems
to be solved. DNA tests reveal
that what we have here is a case of
mistaken identity. The animal that
was killed is a coyote with a very
bad case of mange.

How to Survive in the
DESERT

If you're going to be out chasing the Chupacabra, you'll need to know how to survive in a desert climate. It's hot. It's dry. And if you're not careful, it could kill you. After following the howls of the Chupacabra into the desert on my last trip, I realized I had lost sight of camp. And the hunting party! This is how I survived:

- Make sure you have a hat. Covering your head is a top priority. If the top of your head is exposed to the sun for a long time, your body needs to work harder to keep itself cool.

- Find shade. A cactus, small shrub, rocky outcropping, or ravine will keep you out of the direct sun.

- Don't exert yourself during the day. This will help you conserve water.

- Ration the water. Don't guzzle it. Taking smaller sips throughout the day is better in this survival situation.

- Don't eat. Staying hungry will help you conserve water. The more you eat, the thirstier you'll get.

- Keep cool. Panicking in a survival situation is never good. Stay put and seek shade nearby.

- Make a mark. Use a stick to make an "X" in the sand or on a bush.

- Get cozy. The daytime temperatures in the desert will fry you, but the nighttime temperatures will chill you to the bone. Seek shelter near some rocks, which will release the heat of the day throughout the cold nights.

How do you tell if you're getting dehydrated? Easy. When you pee, look at the color. If it is light yellow, you are hydrated. If it is dark or bright yellow, you could need more water.

Getting lost in the desert is no joke. Make sure you know these basic survival skills or the vultures will be circling for you.

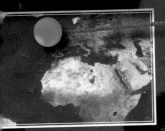

KRAKEN

AUGUST 17, 2013

We have set sail for the coast of Greenland in search of a Kraken. Reports have dwindled since the 1800s, but we have some time, and Greenland is beautiful. The seas are a bit rough today, and I find myself hugging the rail quite a bit. Hopefully, we'll find the evidence we need.

KRAKEN CASE FILE

The Kraken is about 40 ft. to 50 ft. (12 m to 15 m) long, including the tentacles. It has been described as a giant octopus or squid of some sort. It can be found off the coasts of Norway and Greenland. It is said to eat large fish. Wherever it appears, there are bubbles of water, sudden and dangerous currents, and the appearance of new islets.

Kraken

Elephant

Horse

Human

The Legend

The legend started in the late 14th century as people began to expand their horizons and set out on epic adventures across the sea. This is when the Kraken was first classified as a cephalopod.

IT CAPSIZED OUR BOAT!

I have good news and bad news. Our boat was attacked last night by what can only be described as a Kraken. The large tentacles of this massive creature reached out of the water and pulled our boat onto its side. Luckily, we were able to get off a distress signal in time and were rescued by the US Coast Guard within the hour. Boy, were those waters cold! Good thing we had on our wet suits.

Now the bad news. What attacked us was a Giant Squid. We recovered a great deal of evidence on remote beaches in Greenland. We are beginning to suspect that the Giant Squid is indeed what sailors of old referred to as the Kraken.

The giant squid does exist. It is a deep-ocean-dwelling creature that comes to the surface to feed. The largest one ever found measured 59 ft. (18 m) in length and weighed almost a ton (900 kg). Researchers still know little about this creature, though they believe these massive animals are found in all of the world's oceans.

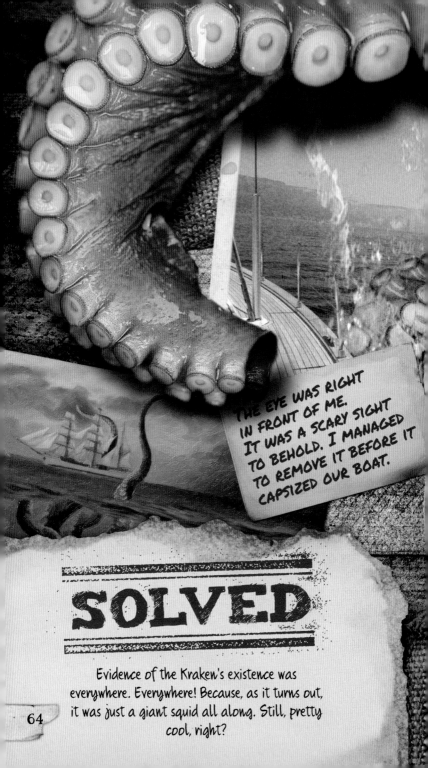

THE EYE WAS RIGHT IN FRONT OF ME. IT WAS A SCARY SIGHT TO BEHOLD. I MANAGED TO REMOVE IT BEFORE IT CAPSIZED OUR BOAT.

SOLVED

Evidence of the Kraken's existence was everywhere. Everywhere! Because, as it turns out, it was just a giant squid all along. Still, pretty cool, right?

How to Survive a
SHIPWRECK

Our boat was capsized, but we were rescued rather quickly. **H**ere's what you need to do if your rescue isn't as quick as ours was.

- Always wear a life preserver when you are out on the water. It will save your life, even if you are a good swimmer.

- Send a distress signal. This could include radio signal, flags, smoke, or flares.

- Get into a lifeboat. If one isn't available, slowly swim to the nearest floating object.

- Wring out any wet clothes. Hypothermia can set in if you don't get yourself dry quickly.

- Create some kind of shelter. Whether you are still at sea or have reached land, create a of shelter with sacks, boxes, or trees.

- Find water. You can collect rainwater and condensation for drinking. DO NOT drink seawater. It will make you even more dehydrated, because your kidneys will need to filter out all of the salt from your blood.

- Finding food. You'll have an easier time of it if you are on land. But, if you are still adrift, eat starches and fats, but very little protein. Proteins require water to digest.

- Conserve your energy. Sleep whenever possible. This will help you maintain your energy levels and reduce dehydration.

We came very close to catching the Kraken, which, in this case, was actually just a giant squid. We'll have to go back to the lab and review the evidence. I need to talk to some marine biologists about the findings. Then, we'll plan our next trip to hunt down this elusive monster, if it's indeed out there...

NEW ZEALAND WILD MAN

Also known as Moehau, Maero, Rapuwai, Tuuhourangi, Taongina, and Matau

May 27, 2012

After an 18-hour flight, we landed on the South Island of New Zealand, in Christchurch. We're exhausted, but need to head out early in the morning to begin our 30-day exploration of New Zealand's back country in search of the Maori legends of the Wild Man.

WILD MAN CASE FILE

The wild men of New Zealand are described as very aggressive and more than happy to kill and eat any human that crosses their path. They are said to resemble humans, but with a lot more body hair, an apelike face, long fingers, and sharp nails. The wild men are said to be between 8 ft. and 11 ft. (2.4 m and 3.4 m) tall.

New Zealand Wild Man

Human

The Legend

There are several different names for the Wild Men of New Zealand. All encounters talk of strong creatures who are cannibalistic in nature. It is likely that these man-beasts may exist in the more remote areas of bush throughout both islands.

The Maori are the indigenous Polynesian people of New Zealand.

On the North Island of New Zealand, you might find the Taonginas. This population of Wild Men were said to attack any fisherman who strayed into their territory. Yet modern encounters with these beasts show them fleeing at the sight of humans.

Legend has it that the Rapuwai were able to crush a strong Maori warrior with ease. These creatures were intelligent and able to make tools out of wood and stone. The Maori legends say that as these Wild Men evolved, they fled to other uninhabited islands of Polynesia.

DUNG SAMPLE FOR TESTING

HAIR SAMPLES FOUND IN THE BEDDING

Our evidence is mounting for the existence of these humanlike monsters. These are the best of all the samples we found.

Locals say that sightings have become fewer and fewer over the years. This could possibly indicate that the species may be on the brink of extinction, or may be extinct already.

BONE TOOLS
FOUND NEAR
THE BEDDING
SITE

IT WAS STANDING RIGHT THERE!

It was unbelievable! The creature, or hairy human, was standing not 5 ft. (1.5 m) from me. I snapped a few photos, but we'll have to see if I got the shot or not. I walked right up on it and didn't even see it. It stood taller than me. I'd guess the height at 6 1/2 ft. (2 m) tall. He threw a few rocks in my direction and took off into the trees. I'm not sure who was more scared—him or me.

COROMANDEL

In the **Karangahake Gorge** in Coromandel, footprints have been found as recently as 2010. It is thought that the largest population of **Wild Men** is found in the **Coromandel Range**.

The creature had these long, crazy nails that looked like sharp talons. I was a little intimidated.

How to Survive a
WILD MAN ATTACK

First, you shouldn't put yourself in the position of being attacked by any wild creature, much less a Wild Man. But sometimes you find yourself in the situation. Here's how I got out when I came face-to-face with one.

- Stay on the marked trails.

- As you walk, talk loudly, call out, or sing. This will scare off any large creature.

- Always go with a companion. There is safety in numbers.

- Never hike at night.

- Store any food in a "safe" container. Wild men have a much better sense of smell than you do.

- Do not make eye contact with the Wild Man. Stand still, stay quiet, and back away slowly.

- Never shout or run away. This usually indicates to the Wild Man that you are prey and should be chased.

- Try to appear larger by opening your jacket or raising your arms or backpack.

We found a lot of evidence to support our theory that the Wild Men of New Zealand are real monsters. However, the proof is not conclusive. We'll have to head back here again soon to further study these monsters.

MONGOLIAN DEATH WORM

or Allghoi Khorkhoi or intestine worm

JULY 10, 2011

We are meeting with Mongolia's nomadic tribesmen today about the rumor of a giant worm that is rarely seen aboveground. Many of us in the expedition are skeptical of this worm's existence, but it is up to us to investigate any monster that is brought to our attention.

MONGOLIAN DEATH WORM CASE FILE

The Mongolian Death Worm looks like a cow's intestine. The tribesmen describe it as being red in color with no idea which is the head and which end is the tail. One tribesman described it as reaching lengths of about 10 ft. (3 m) and weighing as much as 1,000 lbs. (454 kg). This monster lives in the Gobi Desert of Outer Mongolia. It is said that the Death Worm attacks by emitting an electrical charge, like the electric eel, and if that's not bad enough, it also has the ability to use a deadly boiling acid to defend itself.

The Legend

The legends come from the tribesmen that wander the Gobi Desert. The stories tell of animals that simply disappear, and hunting parties that leave with 5 or 6 members, but return with half that many. One story tells of a camel being attacked by the Mongolian Death Worm. The electrical pulse brought the camel to the ground and the acid made it disintegrate. There is mounting evidence of the Death Worm's existence because of the carnage it leaves in its path.

VOLTMETER REGISTERED 1000 VOLTS WHEN NEAR THE MONGOLIAN DEATH WORM

EVIDENCE:
MY T-SHIRT WITH
BURN HOLES.
IT WAS QUITE
THE STRUGGLE.

There is overwhelming evidence to support the theory that the Mongolian Death Worm is real, including burn holes in my shirt from the monster.

A SMALL PART OF THE DEATH WORM WE CAPTURED

GETTING TOO CLOSE TO A MONGOLIAN DEATH WORM

WE GOT ONE!

It didn't take long to get what we came for. It looks more like a reptile than a worm to me, possibly a type of sand boa. It was in the middle of devouring a camel as I slowly approached to register the charge it was giving off. You could hear the electricity crackling in the air. Unfortunately, I was a bit too close as it spat acid that hit my shirt. Luckily, I got the shirt off before the acid touched my skin.

I'm not sure what happened after that. The creature seized suddenly and fell to the ground. We're sending the body off to the cryptozoologists in Oxford, England, for analysis.

An electric eel has a complex nervous system, where each cell acts like a battery. If an eel lived above water, it would turn its body into the equivalent of a 500-volt battery.

The monster stalks prey until the moment is right.

How to Safely Handle a
MONGOLIAN DEATH WORM

Electricity is not something to mess with. It's generally not advisable to capture an electrified monster, but if you have to, like I did, do it carefully. Here are a few things you can do to keep yourself safe:

- Always wear insulated rubber gloves.
- Wear safety goggles.
- Use a net with a very long handle.

This monster gave me the craziest experience in all of my hunting days. Its acidic secretions destroyed my clothes, but I got what I came for in the end...the monster itself. It has been sent off to the lab. We should have the results in the next couple of days.

MOTHMAN

DECEMBER 13, 2013

There have been new sightings of Mothman over the last couple of weeks. Eyewitnesses in West Virginia are afraid that another disaster is about to happen. The last sighting ended with the deaths of 46 people. I'm hoping we get to the bottom of this before anything else happens. We'll be out in the morning to hear these new stories.

MOTHMAN CASE FILE

Mothman is said to be 6.5 ft. to 7 ft. (about 2 m) tall, with a wingspan of 10 ft. (3 m). The shadowy creature was reported flying great distances at speeds up to 100 mph (160 kph). It has red glowing eyes the size of baseballs. One eyewitness said, "The thing scared the living daylights out of me. It was standing right in the middle of the road. Then, it was gone in the blink of an eye."

8'0"
7'0"   Mothman
6'0"
Human
5'0"
4'0"   Mountain
         Gorilla
3'0"
2'0"
1'0"

The Legend

From November 1966 through December 1967, dozens of people reported a huge, semi-human winged creature with glowing red eyes in and around Point Pleasant, West Virginia. Legend says that these sightings were an omen predicting a horrible disaster that happened on December 15, 1967. The Silver Bridge connecting West Virginia with Ohio collapsed into the freezing waters of the Ohio River during rush hour traffic, killing 46 people. Once the bridge collapsed, the reported sightings of the Mothman stopped.

85

COULD SANDHILL CRANES BE MISTAKEN FOR MOTHMAN?

MOTHMAN STATUE IN POINT PLEASANT, WEST VIRGINIA

HISTORIC PHOTO, SILVER BRIDGE COLLAPSE, POINT PLEASANT, WEST VIRGINIA, DECEMBER 1967

We have very little evidence to go on for the Mothman. I would think it was a hoax or a case of mistaken identity for most if not for all of the eyewitness accounts.

COULD THE MOTHMAN REALLY BE A VULTURE?

Cryptozo

WING SAMPLE FOUND BY THE OLD BRIDGE. SENDING TO A LAB FOR ANALYSIS

COULD THE EYES OF THE MOTHMAN HAVE A LIGHT-REFLECTING SURFACE, CALLED A TAPETUM LUCIDUM, SO HE CAN SEE IN THE DARK?

Mothman
and other curious encounters

Mysteriou

Is MOTHMAN Back?

There have been about 20 new sightings of Mothman in different areas of the Northeast in the past couple of weeks. Is it back? Are the prophecies starting all over again?

We're heading out into the field to find this monster or conclude that it's a case of mistaken identity, once and for all.

Eyewitness accounts vary wildly from case to case. Of all the people we came across, the glowing eyes remained consistent in everyone's stories.

SOLVED

We have nothing. I have no idea what these people saw, but I'll bet it was a large bird, possibly a sandhill crane or vulture. There just isn't enough evidence to call it anything else.

ORANG PENDEK

APRIL 17, 2012

We've been called to the island of Sumatra to search for the elusive Orang Pendek, which means "short person" in Indonesian. We'll head off into the jungle tomorrow to see if we can find the evidence that the scientific community needs to consider this little monster a new species.

ORANG PENDEK
CASE FILE

The Orang Pendek is described as being 2 ft. to 5 ft. (.6 m to 1.5 m) tall and walks on two feet. It is covered in gray, brown, or reddish-brown hair. By all accounts it lives on the ground, not in the trees. It is said to have the strength to tear small trees from the ground. The locals described the creature as being vegetarian and isn't normally aggressive, but others have said that the Orang Pendek is very territorial and aggressive. Could this be the missing link, a distant relative of humans?

The Legend

Locals describe a small creature the size of a gibbon, but that lives on the land. Villagers tell tales of some unknown animal that lurks in the shadows of the jungle. The giant panda and the mountain gorilla were thought to exist only in legend until scientists documented them. The Sumatran forests are so dense that the Orang Pendek could be another new species. To date, no specimen has been found, living or dead, and no physical evidence exists, except for some footprints.

MUMMIFIED BODY FOUND IN ORANG PENDEK TERRITORY.

FOOTPRINT CAST OF ORANG PENDEK

ORANG PENDEK ATTACKING OUR MONSTER HUNTING PARTY

There is some debate on whether the Orang Pendek is a new species or a monster. We're still not sure, but we're getting closer to the answer.

MUMMIFED ORANG PENDEK

NEST OF ORANG PENDEK

TOOTH FOUND ON THE GROUND. COULD BE FROM THE ORANG PENDEK.

I WAS HIDING BEHIND A TREE WHEN THESE HANDS APPEARED BESIDE ME.

It Was SMALL!

We trekked farther and farther into the jungles in search of the elusive Orang Pendek. We did see a few gibbons and orangutans that could have been mistaken for an Orang Pendek. But just as we were thinking it was a case of mistaken identity, the little creature came out from behind a tree about 100 yds. (90 m) ahead of us. It was definitely not an orangutan or gibbon.

One of the false positives on our trip was this little gibbon. He was perched very neatly on a post.

We keep seeing a small creature running from behind the trees. The jungle is so dense and dark it's really difficult to see anything.

Endangered Species of SUMATRA

Due to deforestation, farming, illegal trade, and poaching, the following animals are critically endangered:

Sumatran **T**iger - less than 400 left in the wild

Sumatran **E**lephant - less than 3,000 left in the wild

Sumatran **R**hinoceros - less than 400 left in the wild

Orangutan - less than 60,000 left in the wild

Deforestation might be the reason the Orang Penek has been so hard to find! What if it's facing extinction?

In 2007, scientists discovered more than 100,000 Western Lowland Gorillas. Prior to this, we didn't know half of these creatures existed. If 100,000 gorillas can go undetected, isn't it possible that the **Orang Pendek** is just as hidden?

There are other stories of hominid beings on other Indonesian islands as well, including the **Orang Kardil** and the **Ebu Gogo**.

How to Survive in the
JUNGLE

The thick, dark jungles are a monster hunter's worst nightmare. You can barely tell what is in front or behind you. If you're going in search of the Orang Pendek, there are some things you'll need to bring with you. These jungles are home to spiders, snakes, mosquito swarms, and tigers that could end your adventure. Trust me, mosquitoes can be a bigger threat to your health than any monster I've ever hunted. They'll eat you alive! Unless you brush up on these important tips.

Here are a few things to keep in mind:

- Leave your trip schedule with a friend who is not going with you or a forest ranger. If you get lost, they'll know where to start searching.

- Bring a GPS, maps, and compass. I've gotten lost in the jungle before, and it's not the kind of adventure I'd repeat.

- Choose a campsite that is away from trees. Falling trees and branches kill a lot of people in the jungle.

- Protect yourself from mosquitoes. You'll need netting or the sap from a camphor tree.

- Stay out of the water! Crocodiles, leeches, electric eels, anacondas, and piranhas like to hang out there.

- Keep your shoes and clothes as dry as possible. Wet shoes and clothes can lead to bacterial infections.

- If you have to climb a tree or hill to see where you are, don't grab onto the brush or vines. I made that mistake and ended up with a handfull of thorns on my last trip.

- At night, you will need to watch out for creepy crawlies, like ants, snakes, spiders, and scorpions. You'll need to have a shelter that is above the ground to avoid these little beasts. A hammock covered by an A-frame (with a mosquito net) is the best kind of shelter. Don't forget to check your shoes for unwanted visitors before putting them on.

We were sweating bullets trekking through the jungle when this little creature, not more than 3 feet (1 m) tall, jumped out from behind a tree with a spear in hand and scared the living daylights out of us. All of my guides fled, and I stood frozen in fear. I managed to lift my hands into the air and yell at the top of my lungs. The look of surprise on the creature's face was great! It turned tail and ran into the jungle with its little legs really moving.

We'll have to return to see if we can communicate with it next time.

OGOPOGO

OCTOBER 25, 2011

We've arrived in Vancouver, Canada, this evening. We'll stay overnight in the hotel before heading to a campground just off Lake Okanagan. Hopefully, our 21-day expedition will get to the bottom of the recent sightings of the Ogopogo. This creature has plagued the lake for centuries!

OGOPOGO CASE FILE

Ogopogo is a lake monster described by eyewitnesses as a dark, multi-humped creature with green, black, brown, or gray skin. Its head looks like that of a snake. Some say it has ears or horns, others don't mention this feature. Many describe a log that "came to life." Ogopogo is thought to be 40 ft. to 50 ft. (12 m to 15 m) long. It definitely eats fish in the lake, but it has been known to "snatch" animals off the beach, too.

Ogopogo

Human

Horse

Lake Okanagan is 84 mi. (135 km) long and between 2.5 mi. to 3 mi. (4 km to 5 km) wide. It is 840 ft. (256 m) at its deepest.

The Legend

There is an indigenous Canadian legend of a beast, called Naitaka, that would demand sacrifices from travelers for safe passage across Lake Okanagan. In 1926, more than 100 people saw the lake monster. Arthur Folden first captured the creature on film in 1968. A 1991 expedition searched the lake with high-tech devices and sonar looking for any evidence of the creature. Nothing was found, not even carcasses or bones. In 2005, the National Geographic Channel revealed that the object in Folden's film was indeed a real animal. Sightings and cell phone videos continue to this day.

No Doubt About It!

There is no doubt in my mind that what we captured on video is indeed a large creature that lives in Lake Okanagan. It was blackish gray with flashes of green. The head did indeed look like a snake head, and it moved swiftly in the water with the classic humps rising out of the water. Our film is being analyzed now. We may extend our stay to see if we can pick up more evidence. And I can tell you, this was no log.

ESCAPED ANACONDA, MISTAKEN FOR OGOPOGO?

STURGEON, MISTAKEN FOR OGOPOGO?

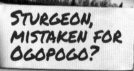

BONE SAMPLE OF OGOPOGO

RIPPLES ON LAKE OKANAGAN, RIGHT BEFORE CATCHING A GLIMPSE OF OGOPOGO

OARFISH ARE EASILY MISTAKEN FOR LAKE MONSTERS.

How to Survive an
OGOPOGO ATTACK

You're out on the lake to do a little fishing. All of a sudden something large bumps your boat. It's like something out of a science-fiction movie.

WHAT YOU DO:

- Always wear a life jacket.
- Do not panic. Panicking will only make matters worse.
- If your boat capsizes, stay with the boat.
- Get out of the water as quickly as possible, even if it's on your upside-down boat. The water steals body heat 25 times faster than air.
- If you can't get out of the water, reach for something that floats, like a cooler or other flotation device.
- Huddle together to stay warm.
- If the river monster attacks you, strike at the eyes and nose areas. These are the most sensitive areas.

I don't know what it is about me and boats. If I'm monster hunting in a boat, I'm bound to get wet. This time was no exception. I ended up swimming back to shore when something tipped my boat over. The idea of swimming in the lake with the Ogopogo still gives me nightmares. I'm lucky I wasn't eaten. Good thing I learned to wear a life jacket after being thrown into Loch Ness Lake. The water was freezing!

BEAST OF BODMIN MOOR (and other Phantom Cats)

APRIL 6, 2010

Livestock have been mauled and killed throughout the moors of Cornwall in England. A recent sighting of the Beast of Bodmin Moor has us scrambling to get our equipment set up and in place to get the evidence needed to prove this cat is real.

Human

Phantom
Cat

Mountain
Gorilla

BEAST OF BODMIN MOOR CASE FILE

The beast is described as a black panther that lives on the moors of Cornwall, in England. Cornwall farmers believe that up to 17 black panthers or dark leopards stalk the area. Its eyes catch the light, which makes them glow. The long scratch marks and bite marks left in the prey are evidence of a big cat.

The Legend

For decades, people on the British Isles have reported sightings of big black cats. Every year, more than 2,000 big-cat sightings are reported throughout Britain, but particularly in Cornwall. The elusiveness of these creatures makes their existence difficult to prove. Experts say there should be more evidence than what has been found.

We've been hunting these sneaky cats on and off for more than 10 years. Here are a few of the better pieces of evidence that we've found in all those years.

SKIN SAMPLE FOUND NEAR THE DEAD COWS.

MOTION SENSOR CAMERA CAPTURED THIS

I know this beast is out there. A large cat will either break its prey's neck by ripping and biting into its flesh and bones, or by suffocating it by putting its mouth over its prey's nose and mouth. Dogs don't kill in this way. The carcasses we've found indicate a big cat of some kind.

PUNCTURE MARK ON HEAD OF A DEER INDICATES A BIG-CAT KILL

Doubt About the Beast of Bodmin Moor

A big cat expert in Tampa, Florida, says that he has doubts about a big cat being released into the wild and surviving. Big predators don't just stay hidden in a while, but every couple of days. Although big cats are very adaptable, there would have to be a lot of prey around to satisfy their hunger.

THAT WAS ONE BIG CAT!

We set up motion sensor cameras and a cat attraction lure where several trails meet. There were also several big-cat tracks in the mud. What we got with our cameras is unbelievable! We may actually have conclusive proof that these big cats do exist.

Animal Killing Livestock in Exmoor

Some animal has killed 80 sheep in Exmoor. Over a few months, there have been more than 200 mutilated bodies of farm animals found on the moors. Royal Marine sharpshooters have been dispatched to the area to locate the beast.

Skull Found Could be the Beast of Bodmin Moor

A 14-year old boy found a big cat skull out on the moors and sent it to the Natural History Museum in London. Scientists concluded that the skull is not one of the common animals on the moors, like badgers or foxes. It is definitely the skull of a big cat.

What to Do if You're
⇨ATTACKED BY A
WILD ANIMAL

What would you do if you came across a big cat on the moors of Britain? It would be the same for any big cat, anywhere.

- Never approach a wild cat (small or large). Give it the time and space to escape.

- Do not bend down or over. You do not want the big cat to think you're easy prey.

- Fall to the ground and roll into a ball with your hands behind your neck. Leave on any backpack that you might be carrying.

- Play dead as long as you can. Wait until the predator is well away before you begin to move.

- If you are bitten or scratched, clean and dress the wounds and seek medical attention immediately.

Having an exotic big cat was all the rage in the 1960s and '70s in Britain. They were kept without regulations. In 1976, the British government passed legislation that made it illegal to own a predatory cat without a very expensive license. Rather than pay the fee, some cat owners freed their dangerous animals. It wasn't illegal to release the pets until 1981. How many cats were released without anyone knowing?

Our evidence is still being reviewed by zoologists at Oxford University, in England. But I have no doubt in my mind that what I saw was a very large black cat running across the moors. No one would be able to convince me otherwise. After all, this is not my first monster-hunting rodeo.

We'll have to get back here soon with a tracker and zoologist. If we can get the large cat tranquilized, perhaps we can solve this monster mystery.

YOWIE

JUNE 18, 2012

We've teamed up with Yowie hunters in Australia to begin our three-month expedition. It is not quite winter in Australia, but it's getting much cooler. Our gear is getting loaded on the trucks for tomorrow's trek into the wilderness. Hopefully, the evidence we find will support a new species discovery.

YOWIE CASE FILE

The Yowie is called different things throughout Australia, including Quinkin, Joogabinna, Jurrawarra, Puttikan, Doolaga, and Gubba. It is described as a hairy, ape-like creature that stands between 7 ft. (2 m) and 12 ft. (3.6 m) tall. A Yowie's feet are much larger than a human's, and its nose is wide and flat. Some reports say the Yowie is shy, but others say it is a very aggressive creature.

Is it a monster or a new species?

Yowie

Alaskan Brown Bear

Human

The Legend

Stories of the Yowie began in the 1800s with reports of apes or hairy men in the woods. There have been hundreds of reported Yowie sightings in New South Wales. Springbrook, in southeast Queensland, has had more Yowie sightings than anywhere else in Australia.

CONFIRMED
YOWIE SKULL

YOWIE BONES

116

FECAL MATTER FOUND NEAR SIGHTINGS. SENDING FOR ANALYSIS

MOTION-SENSOR CAMERA CAPTURED THIS IMAGE OF YOWIE

WE GOT IT ON FILM!

We've been hiking the Springbrook area of southeast Queensland for the last week, and we finally got what we came for, an image of the Yowie. But the price of that photo was high. It came at us out of nowhere and tore at everything, including the camera. It was all we could do to get away.

How to Survive a
YOWIE
ATTACK

After our narrow escape from the Yowie, we have some advice for others attempting to get a photo of this beast. First, it was about 12 ft. (3.7 m) tall. This really surprised us. We were expecting it to be big, but not that big. Second, it caught us by surprise. One minute we were walking along, and the next our team and our gear were scattered across the landscape. We were very lucky. Here's what we would do differently next time:

Focus! Don't let your mind wander. This is how the beast snuck up on us in the first place. We were tired, exhausted, really, from not getting much sleep for the last couple of nights.

1. Remember! You are in Yowie territory. He's not in yours. Be respectful of the area and the power of this beast.

2. Make sure any food is stowed in a bear-safe container. We think the Yowie was after some beef jerky that my cameraman was carrying in his backpack. The pack was torn to shreds and most of the food was gone.

Despite some of our problems on this expedition, we are almost convinced of the existence of the Yowie.

We'll have to return soon to see if our theories hold true, but the evidence we gathered seems to support the fact that what we have here is a real live monster.

MOKELE-MBEMBE

OCTOBER 20, 2013

We landed in Kinshasa to begin our journey. We will hop a small plane to Bumba in the morning. From there, we will hike into the jungle of the Congo River Basin. Our three-week expedition will trek across some dangerous African terrain. All previous expeditions to document the Mokele-Mbembe have failed.

The Legend

Stories of the dreaded Mokele-Mbembe have been around for more than 200 years. All accounts talk of this unidentified dinosaur-like creature, but there has never been any proof of the creature's existence. The first story came from a French missionary. In his observation diary, he claims to have seen enormous footprints from a creature he did not actually see. Many expeditions have headed into the region, but none have found concrete evidence of the Mokele-Mbembe.

Mokele-Mbembe

Elephant

Human

MOKELE-MBEMBE CASE

FILE This legendary water creature has been described as having an elephant-like body with a long neck and tail, and the head is fairly small. It sounds very similar to an extinct dinosaur. It is usually gray or a gray-brown in color. Some local tribesmen talk about tradition and spirit rather than a flesh-and-blood creature.

Mokele-Mbembe means "one who stops the movement of rivers" in the Lingala language.

VERTEBRAE, THOUGHT TO BE
THAT OF MOKELE-MBEMBE,
SENDING TO OXFORD
FOR ANALYSIS

MOKELE-MBEMBE
SKULL FOUND
IN THE
JUNGLES NEAR
A WATERING
HOLE

IT'S HUGE!

We didn't have to get too close to see this enormous
creature. It does indeed look like an extinct sauropod, like
Diplodocus. It seems to be a plant-eater and spends most
of its time in or near the water. And we didn't see just one,
there were two with a baby. There must be more of them.

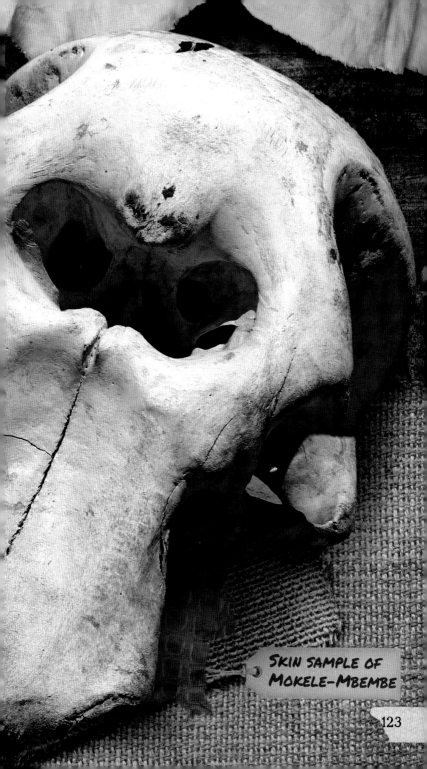

SKIN SAMPLE OF MOKELE-MBEMBE

How to Survive in the
CONGO
RAINFOREST

The Congo rain forest is in Central Africa. **P**eople have lived in this area for thousands of years and have the skills to survive in the harsh environment. **T**hese skills could help you survive not only the dense rain forest, but also the Mokele-Mbembe:

- **W**atch the monkeys. *Anything they eat, you can eat also. Coconuts are your best source of fresh drinking water.*

- **H**eat and humidity are both high in tropical rain forests. *Take care not to wear yourself out. If you need to rest, do so.*

- **W**ear as much clothing as possible. *It will protect you from deadly mosquitoes, leeches, and other creepy crawlies. Inspect your clothes often for these hitchhikers.*

- **W**atch out for hippos. *They kill more people than sharks or crocodiles.*

- **S**tay out of the water as much as possible. *The Mokele-Mbembe has been known to attack dugout canoes, as well as hippos.*

We survived several weeks in the Congo, despite being thrashed by the Mokele-Mbembe tail. That's all the evidence I needed to know. This oversized creature is nothing to trifle with. Next time, we'll take extra precautions. We'll be heading back next month to study the family again.

START YOUR OWN ADVENTURE

Think you're ready to hit the trail and find some monsters? Get started planning your own adventure on these pages. Draw a map of a suspected monster's lair or write up a supply checklist for your next hunt!

Published by Tangerine Press, an imprint of Scholastic Inc; 557 Broadway; New York, NY 10012

10 9 8 7 6 5 4 3 2 1

ISBN 978-0-545-85166-4

Printed and bound in Heshan, China

LINER

Photos ©: Fotolia: push pins (andersphoto), wood background (igor), packaging and masking tape (picsfive), string (Unclesam).

BOOK

Photos ©: cover crocodile eye lenticular: Dennis Stewart; cover dragon scale: TimArbaev/iStockphoto; 2 paper spread and throughout: vlntn/Fotolia; 2 coffee stain and throughout: Nik_Merkulov/Fotolia; 2 polaroid and throughout: Giuseppe Porzani/Fotolia; 2 photo background: aboikis/Fotolia; 2 spider eyes: pelooyen/Fotolia; 2 bat: javarman/Fotolia; 2 cemetery: Tamas Zsebok/Fotolia; 2 stain and throughout: 4khz/iStockphoto; 3 masking tape throughout: picsfive/Fotolia; 3 duct tape and throughout: stuartbur/Fotolia; 3 polaroid and throughout: Andrey Kuzmin/Fotolia; 3 palm branch: rodho/Fotolia; 3 pocket watch: Irochka/Fotolia; 4 paper and throughout: picsfive/Fotolia; 5 string and throughout: Unclesam/Fotolia; 5 paper texture and throughout: photka/Shutterstock, Inc.; 5 deer and throughout: ZoomTeam/Fotolia; 5 mistletoe: Edward Westmacott/Fotolia; 5 house: mimadeo/Fotolia; 5 portrait: katalinks/Fotolia; 5 vintage paper: Scisetti Alfio/Fotolia; 6 push pins and throughout: andersphoto/Fotolia; 6 packaging tape and throughout: picsfive/ Fotolia; 6 map and throughout: Planet Observer/Getty Images; 6 vintage paper and throughout: 719production/Fotolia; 7 coffee stain and throughout: Nik_Merkulov/Fotolia; 7 wood background and throughout: igor/Fotolia; 7 ink drips and throughout: cmeree; 8 woods: quickshooting/Fotolia; 8 leaves: Valentina R./Fotolia; 9 coffee stain and throughout: Nik Merkulov/Fotolia; 10 paper spread and throughout: Ralko/Shutterstock, Inc.; 10 opossum: Tony Campbell/Fotolia; 11 ink stains and throughout: undrey/Fotolia; 11 bat: javarman/Fotolia; 12 , 13 bones: fkienas/iStockphoto; 12 gorilla hand: Scott Rempel/Getty Images; 12 Bigfoot: John Giustina/Corbis Images; 12 forest: Ron Thomas/iStockphoto; 12 wood planks and throughout: Smileus/iStockphoto; 12 toe tags and throughout: Tryfonov/Fotolia; 13 Bigfoot: Roberto A Sanchez/Getty Images; 13 bottom burlap and throughout: yomoyo/iStockphoto; 13 top burlap and throughout: yomoyo/iStockphoto; 13 teeth and throughout: Patrick Jelen/Getty Images; 14 vintage paper and throughout: sveta/ Fotolia; 14 fingerprint and throughout: Sweet Lana/Fotolia; 16 , 17 ice: Lukiyanova Natalia/frenta/Shutterstock, Inc.; 16 paper clip: pixindy/Fotolia; 17 climber: Bartosz Hadyniak/iStockphoto; 17 Mt. Everest: ekashustrova/Fotolia; 18 pick ax and rope: by-studio/ Fotolia; 18 footprints in snow: mjaud/Fotolia; 18 footprint in mud: Juli n Rovagnati/Fotolia; 19 Tibetan statue photo: reborn55/Fotolia; 20 Yeti footprint: Topical Press Agency/Getty Images; 20 wolf teeth: breckeni/iStockphoto; 20 yak: DanielPrudek/iStockphoto; 20 bear claw: wwing/iStockphoto; 24 forest: mimadeo/Fotolia; 25 camping gear: joel 420/Fotolia; 26 foggy night: Zacarias da Mata/ Fotolia; 26 yew branch: cheri131/Fotolia; 26 ring: stockbp/Fotolia; 26 mistletoe: Edward Westmacott/Fotolia; 27 bottle: Szasz-Fabian Erika/Fotolia; 28 wolf canine tooth: Nissa Howard; 28 werewolf hand: calvste/iStockphoto; 28 hair: RobertoDavid/iStockphoto; 28 werewolf in moonlight: Sergey Mironov/Shutterstock, Inc.; 29 human tooth: Patrick Jelen/Getty Images; 29 howling werewolf: PsiProductions/iStockphoto; 29 snarling werewolf: Mi.Ti./Shutterstock, Inc.; 32 old photo frame: Avantgarde/Fotolia; 32 cemetery: datography/Fotolia; 33 full moon ghosts: Alina G/Fotolia; 33 cemetery night: Tamas Zsebok/Fotolia; 33 blood drip: giadophoto/Fotolia; 34 vampire: sumnersgraphicsinc/Fotolia; 34 blood drip: giadophoto/Fotolia; 35 blood drip and throughout: kurapy/Fotolia; 35 Count Dracula: ysbrandcosijn/Fotolia; 35 wound: Todor Rusinov/Fotolia; 36 garlic: Tim UR/Fotolia; 36 briefcase: Winai Tepsuttinun/ Fotolia; 36 mirror: photology1971/Fotolia; 36 flashlight: krasyuk/Fotolia; 36 bottle: Comugnero Silvana/Fotolia; 36 mallet: Gresei/ Fotolia; 37 nails: brunobarillari/Fotolia; 37 vampire set: Uros Petrovic/Fotolia; 37 stake: Uros Petrovic/Fotolia; 40 Plesiosaur bones: Colin Keates/Getty Images; 40 Plesiosaur: Victor Habbick Visions/Science Photo Library/Corbis Images; 41 fish scales: Dennis Kunkel Microscopy, Inc./Visuals Unlimited/Corbis Images; 41 Loch Ness Monster : Dung Vo Trung/Sygma/Corbis Images; 41 dinosaur teeth: Jake Kohlberg/Shutterstock, Inc.; 41 napkin: imagedepotpro/iStockphoto; 43 eel: Juulijs/Fotolia; 43 Whale Shark: frolova elena/Fotolia; 43 owl: Kletr/Fotolia; 44 pen: Rick Henzel/Fotolia; 45 boat: Daniele Pietrobelli/Fotolia; 45 Loch Ness shore: johnbraid/Fotolia; 48 Orangutan: HerminioVeiga/iStockphoto; 48 animal bones: Tphil64/iStockphoto; 49 horse hair: alexandrupetrache/iStockphoto; 49 swamp: sgatlin/iStockphoto; 50 alligator: Pakhnyushchyy/Fotolia; 50 mosquitos: Henrik Larsson/ Fotolia; 50 moss: Big Face/Fotolia; 51 snake: Alexey Kuznetsov/Fotolia; 51 foot: OlegD/Fotolia; 52 , 53 pencil and shavings: lauranovel/Fotolia; 52 swamp: Allen Penton/Fotolia; 53 campsite: Mariusz Blach/Fotolia; 56 coyote fur: andipantz/iStockphoto; 56 cow: Mike Coles/Fotolia; 57 dog: Velar Grant/Demotix/Corbis Images; 57 nails: Raf0007/iStockphoto; 58 cactus: Dmitry/Fotolia; 59 top desert: maurosessanta/Fotolia; 59 bottom desert: Jenitoto/Fotolia; 59 cup: Mike/Fotolia; 62 man in boat: Photobank/Fotolia; 62 octopus tentacles: Vitaly Korovin/Fotolia; 62 seaweed: tempakul/Fotolia; 63 Iceland bay: larrul/Fotolia; 63 squid eye: hiphoto39/ Fotolia; 63 squid tentacles: hiphoto39/Fotolia; 64 gray tentacle: Sprint/Corbis Images; 64 pink tentacle: John Block/Blend Images/ Corbis Images; 64 boat edge: Image Source/Kris Graves RM/cultura/Corbis Images; 64 Kraken painting: John Lund/Blend Images/ Corbis Images; 65 squid eye: Norbert Wu/Science Faction/Corbis Images; 66 forest shelter: daseaford/Fotolia; 67 man: Milles Studio; 67 woman: bonninturina/Fotolia; 70 hair: Louie Psihoyos/Corbis Images; 70 tools: Nathan Benn/Ottochrome/Corbis Images; 70 manure: Wylius/iStockphoto; 70 plastic bag and throughout: audriusmerfeldas/iStockphoto; 71 wild man: Philippe Chevreuil/Corbis Images; 72 rocks: blackboard1965/Fotolia; 73 Karangahak gorge: pink candy/Fotolia; 73 monkey: duelune/Fotolia; 75 eyes: Hektor2/ Fotolia; 78-79 worm: Pete Oxford/Minden Pictures/Corbis Images; 78 voltmeter: StanRohrer/iStockphoto; 78 burn holes: RusN/ iStockphoto; 78 shirt: bonetta/iStockphoto; 79 78,79: Seth Resnick/Science Faction/Corbis Images; 80 worm: kzww/Fotolia; 81 eel: Stacey Newman/iStockphoto; 82 glove: Nomad Soul/Fotolia; 83 net: Lenan/Fotolia; 83 worms: fotomaster/Fotolia; 83 yellow worm: missisya/Fotolia; 83 man: Oleg Zabielin/Fotolia; 86 mothman statue: The Washington Post/Getty Images; 86 transparent wing: Wim van Egmond/Visuals Unlimited/Corbis Images; 86 bridge collapse: Bettmann/Corbis Images; 86 crane: ElementalImaging/iStockphoto; 86 vulture: rruntsch/iStockphoto; 87 books: Portland Press Herald/Getty Images; 87 raccoon: Mark L Stephenson/Corbis Images; 89 film: Teodora D/Fotolia; 92-93 mummified monkey: DEA/W. Buss/Getty Images; 92-93 bedding: Education Images/Getty Images; 92 jungle: PacoRomero/iStockphoto; 92 orangutan hands: ShantiHesse/iStockphoto; 92 footprint cast: Barcroft Media/Getty Images; 93 tooth: fkienas/ iStockphoto; 94 White Checked Gibbon: bereta/Fotolia; 95 bamboo jungle: frog-travel/Fotolia; 95 Batak house: Alice Nerr/Fotolia; 95 Mt. Kerinci forest: feathercollector/Fotolia; 96 elephant: johny87/Fotolia; 96 Sumatran Tiger: Darren Green/Fotolia; 96 orangutan: jodie777/Fotolia; 96 Sumatran Rhino: neelsky/iStockphoto; 97 photo frame: Avantgarde/Fotolia; 97 gorillas: wildnerdpix/Fotolia; 97 tape frame: picsfive/Fotolia; 98 explorer: stokkete/Fotolia; 102-103 poster: wwing/iStockphoto; 102-103 oarfish: The Asahi Shimbun/Getty Images; 102 boat on lake: Darrel Giesbrecht/Getty Images; 102-103 dinosaur bones: Louie Psihoyos/Corbis Images; 102 sturgeon: Matthias Breiter/Minden Pictures/Corbis Images; 102 anaconda: Jason Edwards/ National Geographic Creative/Corbis Images; 102 Barosaurus bone: DK Limited/ Corbis Images; 105 paddle and jacket: Marek/Fotolia; 108 cat claw: Jebb Harris/ Zuma Press/Corbis Images; 108 panther: Enjoylife2/iStockphoto; 109 deer skull: Axel Ganguin/Westend61/Corbis Images; 110 sheep: jodie777/Fotolia; 111 panther eyes: Eric Gevaert/Fotolia; 111 tiger: art9858/Fotolia; 113 tigers: stifos/Fotolia; 113 pencil: Juli n Rovagnati/Fotolia; 116-117 rainforest: Petershort/iStockphoto; 116 bones: gcoles/iStockphoto; 117 manure: LPETTET/iStockphoto; 118 Queensland Rainforest: THPStock/Fotolia; 119 kangaroos: clabert/iStockphoto; 119 rucksack: burne111/Fotolia; 122-123 crocodile skin: belterz/iStockphoto; 122-123 skull: Bernhard Richter/iStockphoto; 122 tooth: Ryan M. Bolton/Shutterstock, Inc.; 124 palm fronds: rodho/Fotolia; 124 statue sketch: Les Cunliffe/Fotolia; 124 woman in boat: NLPhoto/Fotolia; 125 hippo: JohanSwanepoel/Fotolia; 127 forest shelter: daseaford/Fotolia; 127 vampire set: Uros Petrovic/ Fotolia; 128 Mt. Everest: ekashustrova/Fotolia; 128 paddle and jacket: Marek/Fotolia.